CELEBRATING
CINCO DE MAYO

BY ANN HEINRICHS · ILLUSTRATED BY KATHLEEN PETELINSEK

The Child's World®
childsworld.com

Published by The Child's World®
1980 Lookout Drive • Mankato, MN 56003-1705
800-599-READ • www.childsworld.com

ISBN 9781503853812 (Reinforced Library Binding)
ISBN 9781503854628 (Portable Document Format)
ISBN 9781503855007 (Online Multi-user eBook)
LCCN: 2021953061

Printed in the United States of America

ABOUT THE AUTHOR
Ann Heinrichs lives in Chicago, Illinois. She has written more than two hundred books for children. She loves traveling to faraway places.

ABOUT THE ILLUSTRATOR
Kathleen Petelinsek is a freelance illustrator in the Minneapolis area. She has loved to draw since childhood.

CONTENTS

CHAPTER 1

Long Live Mexico!

Floats and marching bands move down the street. Cars are honking their horns. And everyone's waving colorful flags. It's *Cinco de Mayo* (SEEN-koh day MY-oh)!

Cinco de Mayo is a Mexican holiday. Cinco de Mayo is Spanish for "the fifth of May." That's when this festival takes place. It's a time to celebrate Mexican **pride**.

Would you like to learn a Cinco de Mayo greeting? Just say *"Viva México"* (VEE-vah MEH-hee-koh). That means "Long Live Mexico!"

Wave a flag! Join a parade!
It's Cinco de Mayo!

5

CHAPTER 2

What Happened on Cinco de Mayo?

Mexico once belonged to Spain. The Mexican people won their freedom in 1821. But their troubles were not over.

France invaded Mexico in 1862. People in the city of Puebla were brave. They got ready for battle. Many had no guns. Some had nothing but farm tools.

On May 5, fierce fighting broke out. There were many more Frenchmen than Mexicans. But the Mexicans won the battle!

Benito Juárez was the president of Mexico during the Battle of Puebla. On Cinco de Mayo, people sometimes shout *"¡Viva Juárez!"*

Mexican forces at Puebla fought bravely in 1862.

September 16 is Mexican Independence Day. This is when Mexico won independence from Spain.

7

CHAPTER 3

Proud to Be Mexican

Mexicans are proud on Cinco de Mayo. They think about the Battle of Puebla. The people of Puebla fought hard that day. They beat a much larger army. They proved Mexicans are brave and strong.

Cinco de Mayo reminds Mexicans to be proud.

Fiesta Broadway is held in Los Angeles, California. It's the world's biggest Cinco de Mayo festival.

Cinco de Mayo is especially popular in Mexico and in the southwestern United States.

Cinco de Mayo is often celebrated in states near the Mexican border. That includes California, Arizona, New Mexico, and Texas.

People in Mexico celebrate Cinco de Mayo. It's a national holiday there. But it's an even bigger holiday for Mexican Americans. They celebrate their Mexican roots that day. They show how proud they are!

CHAPTER 4

Fiesta Time!

Cinco de Mayo is *fiesta* (fee-ESS-tah) time. Fiesta is Spanish for "festival." Cinco de Mayo is a great day for a parade!

What will you see? You'll see children and grown-ups in colorful costumes. Some are dancing. And some carry Mexican flags. Marching bands go by. They play horns and drums.

You'll see floats covered with hundreds of flowers. There may be fire trucks and people on horseback. City leaders join in, too. Everyone waves to the crowd!

THE COCKROACH
Pancho Villa was a famous Mexican general. He rode in a rickety carriage. His troops called it *la cucaracha* (lah koo-kuh-RAH-chah). That means "the cockroach"! "La Cucaracha" became a popular tune. It's often played by Mexican bands.

La Cucaracha

Spanish:
La cucaracha, la cucaracha
Ya no puede caminar.
Porque no tiene,
Porque le falta
Una pata para andar.

English:
The cockroach, the cockroach
Can't travel anymore.
Because he doesn't have,
Because he lacks
A foot to walk with.

CHAPTER 5

Mexican Costumes

You'll see colorful costumes on Cinco de Mayo. Often they are green, white, and red. Why? Because those are the colors of the Mexican flag!

Cinco de Mayo colors remind us of the Mexican flag.

The Mexican men's costume is called a *charro* (CHAH-roh) suit. A charro is a traditional Mexican horseman.

15

A fan, shawl with fringe, and flowers are part of traditional Cinco de Mayo dress for girls.

Girls and women wear big skirts with ruffles. They wear bright flowers in their hair. And they may carry beautiful fans. Many wear shawls with fringe.

If you're a boy, Cinco de Mayo clothes include a sombrero and a fancy jacket.

Boys and men wear *sombreros* (sohm-BRER-ohz). Those are big Mexican hats. Their jackets and pants have fancy designs. **Spurs** jingle on their shiny black boots.

CHAPTER 6

Music, Dance, and Food

Cinco de Mayo festivals are great fun. People enjoy Mexican music, dance, and food.

Mariachi (mah-ree-AH-chee) bands are playing. The musicians wear traditional Mexican suits. They play trumpets, guitars, and violins. Mariachis may play on a stage. Or they may stroll around.

Dancers put on Mexican **folk dance** shows. They are exciting! The dancers swirl around. They clap their hands and use their feet to tap out a lively beat. Each Mexican state has its own special dances. Each has a special costume, too.

Cinco de Mayo is filled with the music of mariachi bands.

Favorite Mexican Foods

enchiladas (en-chee-LAH-dahs)
tortillas wrapped around a
filling and covered with sauce

mole (MOH-lay)
a hot sauce made with
chilies and chocolate

salsa (SAHL-sah)
a hot sauce made with
tomatoes and chilies

tortillas (tor-TEE-yahs)
round, flat bread

Food stands serve delicious Mexican foods. Many foods are made with hot chili peppers. They are very spicy!

CHAPTER 7

Children's Fun

Children enjoy many games at fiesta time. The *piñata* (peen-YAH-tah) is a favorite. A piñata is shaped like an animal. It's filled with candy. Then it's hung up high overhead.

How do you get the candy? That's the fun part! Someone puts a **blindfold** over your eyes. You are spun around in circles. Then you get a stick.

You swing the stick, trying to hit the piñata. When you hit it—WHACK! The candy comes spilling out. Then children gather up their treats!

PIÑATA SONG

Spanish:
Dale, dale, dale,
no pierdas el tino
porque si lo pierdes,
pierdes el camino.

English:
Hit it, hit it, hit it.
Don't lose your aim
Because if you lose it,
You will lose your way.

Take a swing at the piñata! It's time to celebrate Cinco de Mayo!

BAJEN LA PIÑATA

Spanish:
Bajen la piñata,
Bájenla un tantito,
Que le den de palos
Poquito a poquito.

English:
Lower the piñata,
Lower it a little,
So that they can hit it
Little by little.

CHAPTER 8

Come to Puebla!

Suppose you are in Mexico. Cinco de Mayo is coming. Where is a good place to be? In the city of Puebla! People there are proud of their city. It played a big part in Mexican history.

Mexican soldiers march in parades. They honor the heroes of Mexican wars. Other people march in costume. They wear clothing of the 1860s. This is a reminder of the Battle of Puebla.

Later, there's a big show. People act out the famous battle. Some are dressed like French soldiers. Others dress like the Mexicans. Rifles fire and cannons roar. At last, the Mexicans win. Then it's time for music and food!

JOINING IN THE
SPIRIT OF CINCO DE MAYO

* Do you know Mexican Americans in your school or neighborhood? Ask how their families or communities celebrate Cinco de Mayo.

* Is there a Mexican neighborhood in your city? Does it hold a Cinco de Mayo festival? If so, go and enjoy the sights and sounds!

* Visit a Mexican restaurant for Cinco de Mayo. What colors are the decorations? Why are these colors used?

MAKING POLVORONES
(MEXICAN SUGAR COOKIES)

What you need:
2 cups flour
3/4 cup sugar
1/2 teaspoon cinnamon
1 cup butter or margarine

Directions

1. Preheat the oven to 300 degrees Fahrenheit.*

2. Mix the flour, sugar, and cinnamon in a bowl.

3. In another bowl, whip the butter (or margarine) with an egg beater until it's soft and creamy.

4. Gradually stir in your mixture of flour, sugar, and cinnamon.

5. Using a teaspoon, place about twenty-four small pieces of dough onto an ungreased cookie sheet.

6. Bake for 25 minutes.

7. Allow the cookies to cool before serving.

8. For an even sweeter treat on May 5, sprinkle the warm cookies with any leftover sugar and cinnamon.

*Have an adult help you operate the oven.

MAKING A MEXICAN BIRD RATTLE

What you need:

1 toilet paper roll
1 Popsicle stick
Masking tape
Markers or crayons
Glue
Scissors

2 googly eyes
A handful of small rocks,
    dried beans, or unpopped
    popcorn kernels
Red, orange, yellow, blue,
    and green construction
    paper or colorful feathers

Directions

1. Cover one end of the toilet paper roll with masking tape.

2. Tape the Popsicle stick to the other end of the toilet paper roll. This will be your handle. Use lots of tape so it won't fall off!

3. Put the small rocks, beans, or popcorn kernels inside the toilet paper roll.

4. Cover the open end of the toilet paper roll with masking tape.

5. Cut a piece of red construction paper the same size as the toilet paper roll.

6. Glue the red construction paper around the outside of the toilet paper roll.

7. Cut feather-shaped pieces of blue, yellow, or green construction paper. You can also use real feathers if you have them.

8. Glue the colorful paper or feathers to the outside of the toilet paper roll.

9. Cut a beak shape from the orange construction paper and attach it to the front of the toilet paper roll (opposite the Popsicle stick handle).

10. Glue a googly eye to the toilet paper roll on each side of the beak.

Now you're ready to shake your maraca and celebrate Cinco de Mayo. *Olé!*

GLOSSARY

blindfold (BLIND-fold)—a cloth tied around the head to cover the eyes

folk dance (FOLK DANSS)—a type of dance that is unique to a particular area or group

pride (PRYD)—a feeling of being proud

spurs (SPURZ)—a spiked wheel on the back of a boot

traditional (tru-DISH-uh-null)—following long-held customs

LEARN MORE

BOOKS

Bullard, Lisa. *Marco's Cinco de Mayo.*
Minneapolis, MN: Millbrook Press, 2012.

Cox, Judy. *Cinco De Mouse-O!* New York, NY:
Holiday House, 2010.

Otto, Carolyn. *Celebrate Cinco de Mayo.*
Washington, DC: National Geographic Kids, 2008.

Reader, Jack. *The Story Behind Cinco de Mayo.*
New York, NY: PowerKids Press, 2020.

Sebra, Richard. *It's Cinco de Mayo!*
Minneapolis, MN: Lerner Publications, 2017.

WEBSITES

Visit our website for links about Cinco de Mayo and other holidays:
childsworld.com/links

Note to Parents, Teachers, and Librarians: We routinely verify our Web links to make sure
they are safe and active sites. So encourage your readers to check them out!

INDEX